Soggypaw Siberian Huskies

Big Soggypaw wags to you! ♡
L.A. Adamson

SOGGYPAW SIBERIAN HUSKIES

BY L.A. ADAMSON

L.A. Adamson

This book is based on a true story.

All black and white illustrations are sketched from actual photographs.

SOGGYPAW SIBERIAN HUSKIES

BY L.A. ADAMSON

L.A. Adamson

Copyright © 2012 by L.A. Adamson
All rights reserved.
Printed in the U.S.A.

No part of this book may be copied, stored in a
retrieval system, or duplicated in any form
without the prior written permission of the publisher or author,
except by a reviewer who may quote brief passages to be printed in a
newspaper, magazine or journal.

Copyright © 2012 by TJMF Publishing

Printed and Bound in the United States By
Publisher's Graphics, LLC

Illustrations by Mark Adamson
Cover design by Mark Adamson
Edited by Patty Zion

ISBN Number: 098-29447-5-6
13-digit ISBN Number: 978-0-9829447-5-2
Library of Congress Number: 2012945511

TJMF Publishing

ACKNOWLEDGEMENTS

For my wonderful, animal loving daughter Tonya. You will always be my greatest accomplishment.

Thank you to my family and friends for your patience during my commitment to writing this book.

L.A. Adamson

Contents

INTRODUCTION 7
FOREVER HOME 9
TRAINING IS FUN 19
PRETTY PRINCESS CALENDAR GIRL 27
MIRAGE 37
COW BELLY GIRL 49
THE BIG MOVE 61
UNIQUE NAMES 71
PREPARING FOR THE RACE 85
A MAGICAL EXPERIENCE 99

L.A. Adamson

INTRODUCTION

Hello there, two-legger. I am a Siberian husky dog, and I have a wonderful story to tell you about the Siberian husky breed, my family, and why every dog needs training.

My story begins with Pupp, a former military man from Pennsylvania, searching Florida for a southern girl to settle down with. After a couple of years of what Pupp called scorching heat and unfriendly people, he met that perfect someone. He threw out the bait and caught her, hook, line and sinker. They are admirable, animal-loving people that have been happy together since 1995.

They moved to west central Pennsylvania to be in cooler temperatures and to surround themselves with kind people that wave when you drive by. The plan was to purchase some acreage, fence it in, and encircle their lives with a Siberian husky family.

Well, they managed to get most of it. I will back up a few years and continue this story from my outlook as a young husky.

L.A. Adamson

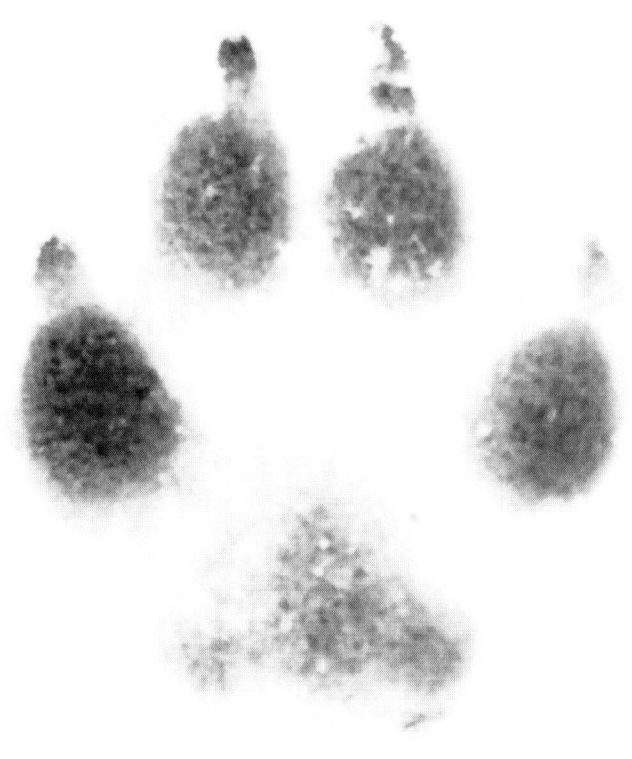

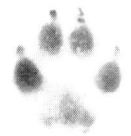

CHAPTER ONE
FOREVER HOME

Born in an AKC (American Kennel Club) breeder's kennel with many other puppies, I was cared for by my mother, Koyuk, a red and white, amber-eyed husky. And, by my pure white great-grandmother, Anevay, whose eyes were a dreamlike ice blue in color. Their names are Native American and usually have a special meaning. Anevay means "superior," and Koyuk is the name of a village in Alaska. Huskies want to be special and without a doubt want a meaning in life, which includes a unique name.

Koyuk and Anevay were great teachers. They educated the puppy litters to obey rules and be kind to all, preparing us for forever homes. Otherwise, we would romp around all day, jump on each other, tug on tails, and take turns trying to pin down the loser of our rivalries.

My brother and I cracked up as we gathered and hid the clan's sticks and straw pieces in a cubbyhole. When our mother inspected our activities for the day, she found our cubbyhole stash; we were relieved when she didn't tell the other puppies.

Then it was bedtime; we curled up in Koyuk's midriff and neck, always touching for comfort.

The next morning, I woke up to the voices of children wanting to buy a puppy.

One by one, I had watched my siblings and playmates embark to forever homes with their new families. I rarely had the chance to say goodbye. Before long, I realized I was the last puppy. I felt sad and all alone, so I stayed hidden in the back corner of the kennel with the idea no one wanted me.

Anevay sensed my broken heart. With her tranquil voice, she spoke sincerely about my special qualities and how I cast a colorful rainbow on everything around me. She said, *"Describing your unique features would take all day. You will soon secure a forever home. Besides, I am the lucky one, as I am allowed a few more days to nurture and adore you. When you are chosen and leave me behind, always remember my love for you is unbroken. I will be with you forevermore."*

We snuggled together as she revealed all her secrets and conditioned my spirit for the outside world. It is clear, we have a divine connection. I no longer felt alone.

Two days later a pair of pretty ladies came to the kennel searching for a husky puppy. One was talking to the other and said, "Pupp has a dream of driving a sled team of huskies. I must find a favorable one for his birthday to help get him started."

While the elder lady was looking at Anevay, the younger lady saw me rolling in a haystack. We made visual contact. She observed me closely. I stared for a moment and was actively drawn to her.

After a gentle stroke of her hand under my chin, I was lifted off the ground and cuddled in her neck. Her feet shuffled toward the other lady as she smiled at me and said, "Hello, my name is Mupp, and this is Grandma. You are so cute. Would you like to live with me and Pupp? You are the perfect birthday present."

"Oh, yes! I would love a forever home with you," I cried.

Mupp passed me to Grandma and said, "Look at her beautiful eyes, Grandma. They are brown, but the left eye is partially blue. That one is called a parti eye."

"She has a fancy mask on her face, too." Grandma said. "Beautiful, cute as can be."

I was kindly returned to the kennel floor. I ran fast to

Anevay and Koyuk, showering them with hugs, kisses, and gratitude for all they had done for me. Anevay said, *"You will have a bountiful life, and in the near future, we will cross paths again, my dear. Remember, together forevermore in our hearts."*

Mupp delivered comfort to Anevay and Koyuk by saying, "Goodbye, Anevay. Goodbye, Koyuk. It was a pleasure to meet you both. Your little girl is in sound hands. Pupp and I will give her perfect care, I promise."

Koyuk was happy to see me go to a forever home of my own, knowing I was starting a whole new life. She gave me a wink, held her head high, and independently marched onward.

As Mupp carried me on her shoulder, I stared at Anevay's beautiful blue eyes, having flashbacks, remembering all the wonderful times we spent together, until she slowly faded away.

I was stricken with grief. Would I ever see my great-grandmother or my mother again? Mupp held me in her lap while Grandma drove and eventually calmed my crying by talking to me about being a homemaker—that she will always be there to care for me. Mupp said, "We don't have any young children of our own. Therefore, you will always be our baby." She continued by describing Pupp and his work as an electrician, how he maneuvers wire and puts boxes together to make lights come on and household accessories work. At the same time, she rubbed behind my ears and scratched my belly. Mupp was so warm and friendly. At half a shake, I was in love.

Next thing I knew, the car stopped and Mupp said in a happy voice, "We're here!" They gathered their belongings, carried me in the house, and set me on the floor.

It was a big house, from my point of view. And an older home that smelled of wood from the timber floors and fresh paint due to Mupp's recent remodeling of the living room.

I have to admit, I was a little scared, and when I'm scared I get the hiccups. Mupp detected my fear and said, "Aw, she has the puppy-cups. Don't be nervous, honey; this is your forever home with lots of new things to explore."

So, I continued sniffing and uncovered the sweet smell of cake in the oven. I also found a glossy kitchen floor to slide across. Mupp giggled as I slid into the stove, messing up the rug and knocking over her soda bottles. I guess you could say it sounded a lot like a bowling alley in the kitchen. That was how I found out that jumping on an empty soda bottle makes a loud noise as it bounces off all four walls.

Soon after, I mastered the challenge of thieving the lids off the empty bottles. As a special treat, Mupp tightened the cap on an empty peanut butter jar and watched me go to work.

Sliding across the kitchen floor.

I had that cap off in less than a minute and could get all the peanut butter out by extending my extra-long tongue to the bottom. Mmm, I like peanut butter, and Mupp liked the funny faces I made when I tried to get it off the roof of my mouth.

After my snack and cheerful humor with Mupp, I began to accept an awareness of security. This forever home was unlike the kennel; I had carpet to lie on, stairs to climb, and window sills to stand on so I could look outside. "Puppy, get down," Grandma suggested.

"Oops, I suppose I shouldn't stand on the window sills," I thought. *"I could fall and hurt myself."*

"You are a little investigator," Grandma said. "We will teach you things you shouldn't do in the house. You have a lot to learn, but you'll be really happy here."

A tiny bit later, Grandma said, "Pupp is home from work."

I thought I heard a different voice from not so far away. As Pupp walked in the door, Mupp picked me up and gently placed me into Pupp's hands. They cheered, "Surprise! Happy birthday!"

Pupp held me up in front of his face, gave me a big smile, and said, "Oh boy, you are so perfect."

Exploring my new world.

"No, no," I told him. *"I am a girl."*

Pupp held me close, kissed my cheek, and explained, "I will name you after Czar, a strong, noble husky I had as a boy. In memory of my grandmother, you will have the middle name, Mae. I will call you Czarah Mae."

I showed my approval by poking my mug into his right eye. Then I told him, *"I will be proud to carry this name; I have a great-grandmother myself."*

Pupp understood, and with his right eye closed, he said, "Thank you for the eye-socket love, Czarah. I love you, too."

It was a wonderful day! The humans were having cake and ice cream, and I was the life of the party.

Meeting Pupp for the first time.

Afterwards, Grandma had to go home, but said she would be back every Sunday night to give me hugs, kisses, and her special treats.

At this point, I decided to nap. I was tired from all the excitement.

When I woke, Mupp and Pupp took me toy shopping at the pet store. There were all kinds of dog toys: big toys, little toys, scary spider toys, and toys that squeak or grunt. The apple of my eye was long, brown colored, half worm and half dog, with a squeaker inside. I named it Worm Dog.

Oops, I didn't mean for that to happen.

While shopping, Mupp found a beautiful gem collar and a matching leash. She clipped the leash onto the collar, slipped it over my head, and set me on the floor. With a gentle tug of the leash, Mupp said, "Come, Czarah, let's walk."

I didn't like this *thing* around my neck. I screamed at her, *"Take it off!"*

Quickly, I pulled backward, the collar slid over my head, and with a bountiful hop, I was on my way to scamper throughout the store, while Mupp and Pupp gave chase. I was having fun until I saw a mad look on their faces. So I quickly stopped! Pupp leaped into the air to keep from stepping on me, and bang! Right into a chow-chow shelf, he soared. Chow-chow flew everywhere.

As Pupp collected himself, he said, "Where are the puppy training books? We need to teach Czarah some rules."

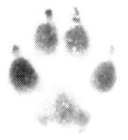

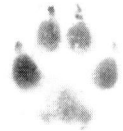

CHAPTER TWO
TRAINING IS FUN

After finding some great educational books for huskies, Mupp and Pupp agreed to take turns teaching me right from wrong. Training meant lots of fun; I would learn many things and get goodies for obeying the rules.

So, every week when Pupp came home from work, he brought me a fresh, tasty surprise to train for and a fashionable toy to keep me busy. Because when I look for things to do, they are not always the right things to do.

Some things were irresistible. I had a problem chewing on Pupp's socks, taking Mupp's full soda bottles, and nipping Pupp on the nose with my sharp needle teeth. It was hard learning right from wrong. I didn't know it was wrong until I was told, and then sometimes, I just couldn't help myself.

Pupp had no doubt that a three-foot-high door gate would keep me in my room when they were away or busy and couldn't watch me. After Pupp secured me, he went into the bathroom to shave and bathe. He worked hard all day and was a stinky Pupp.

Gated in my room, I waited, and waited, and waited. He had been in there a long time. I missed Pupp *very* much while he was in the bath. *So* much that I would dig a hole in the wall to find him.

I dug, and scratched, and dug, and scratched, and chewed. Whew, this made me tired. I needed a drink of water and a nap.

I was sleeping soundly when I heard, "Czarah Mae! What have you done? No, bad girl! You cannot tear a hole in the wall." Pupp was shouting. Yes, I knew I was in trouble again, especially when I heard my middle name. I only wanted my Pupp to come out and play.

Pupp's loud voice scared me. As I backed away, Pupp picked me up, gave me big hugs and kisses, and then talked to me about why it was bad to dig a hole in the wall that he had to fix. He said, "I'm sorry I yelled. I didn't mean to scare you. When we scold you, it is part of your training. This is how you learn." I gave him some socket love; he laughed and gave me more hugs.

I promised to never dig a hole in the wall again, and Pupp promised to never yell at me again. From that moment on, he said the word no, in a soft, but strict tone.

Therefore, instead of causing damage when I got lonely, I frolicked with my toys and made goofy faces to get Mupp's and Pupp's attention. My bat face was the best. I would press my nose against the gate or a window and pull my head down. My upper lip would rise, giving it the look of a bat face. It's really funny; you should try it. I continued to exhibit plenty of comedy throughout my days; it's good for the soul.

During another day's training, Pupp was teaching me a new trick—how to turn a glove inside out to remove treats from the fingertips. It took me a while, but kept me busy.

Mupp's plans were to clean the house that day. She picked up the soggy glove and said, "Pupp, can you please train Czarah in her room for a while?"

Pupp said, "Sure, Czarah, room!" I kindly took the glove from Mupp's hand and went to my room to actively gnaw on the slimy leather. Pupp gated us in, confining us to the best place in the house, a room full of squeaky, drooling entertainment, and the training continued.

After a few minutes, I heard a knock on the front door. It was Grandma; she came to ask Pupp to do some electrical work at her house. So, I jumped over the gate to visit with her

This is my silly bat face.

and realized how much fun that was. So, I jumped over it several more times. Mupp gazed at Pupp and said, "Oh well, there goes all of our confidence in the trustworthy gate."

Jumping made me thirsty. I don't know why, but even my feet wanted water. Without a second thought, I put them into the water dish. I thought this was quite soothing. Mupp seemed to accept this until I splashed the water out of my dish and onto the floor. I was shown the mess and told, "No," as Mupp mopped up the water and refilled my dish. I said thank you with a nod of my head and a glance into her eyes. She understood and smiled.

After my odd misbehaving, it was time for my walk. Without delay, I had an uncontrollable, crazy idea to stop, drop, and roll in a fresh mud puddle. Looking embarrassed, Mupp continued the walk even though I was covered in muddy water. This is why they gave me the nickname Soggypaw, because of my love for water.

It wasn't long before Pupp was home from helping Grandma. I knew it was him by the sound of his truck. The first thing he did when he came in the house was sit on the floor. "Game on," is what Pupp says when it's time for recreation. I started running very fast, then I leaped into

Clearing the trustworthy gate.

the air, and Pupp caught me. He laughed as I pushed him over. We love to romp, and after an intense game or two, plus a mud puddle roll, I tend to get clammy in the armpits.

Pupp said running and training had made me a stinky puppy. It was time for my first bath. Mupp told him about the roll in the mud puddle and how that must have added to my stink. Pupp prepared soapy water in the kitchen sink to a perfect temperature. As he began to place me in the foamy water, my legs stretched out with cat-like paws, kicking up water and fighting him until he arranged my feet to stand up straight.

What was this? It was wet like my drinking water and made me feel heavy. Yuck! It didn't taste like my drinking water. The floating bubbles sparkled and then popped when I touched them with my nose. This bath wasn't so bad; I liked all the scratching and rubbing, mainly behind my ears.

During the rinse cycle, Pupp had the water a little too cold. I began to shiver. He wrapped a big, warm towel around me and held me like a baby, lightly rubbing me dry. Suddenly, I heard a loud noise. Here came Mupp with the blow dryer. Pupp began to laugh and said, "Mupp, Czarah is not going to let you blow dry her." Just then, my fur began to fly, creating tumbleweed fur balls. Pupp brushed me while Mupp blow dried.

Soggypaw Siberian Huskies

Game on, with Pupp.

Puppies don't like baths.

I liked the blow dryer; it made me a fluffy husky. But it sure was warm. I couldn't wait to lie in front of the fan to cool down, chew on an ice cube and take a quick nap.

Chasing my ice cube.

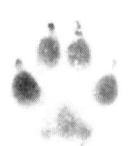

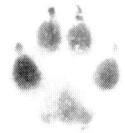

CHAPTER THREE
PRETTY PRINCESS CALENDAR GIRL

After my nap, I was strolling through the house and found another husky behind the bedroom door. It was a girl, just like me. I sniffed her, and at the same time, she sniffed me. I pulled my ears back, and she did too. I wagged my tail, and she did too. I stuck my tongue out, and she did too. Then, I barked, *Boof,* and she did too. This dog copied every move I made.

Just as the dog began to annoy me, Mupp came into the room to see what I was doing and laughed out loud, saying, "Czarah, this is not another dog. It's you in a mirror and called a reflection." Well, I felt like the dumb one. How was I to know? I was just a puppy.

L.A. Adamson

Look, it's another husky!

Sometimes, I went back to the mirror to check myself out, to make sure there was no fur making a beeline for the ceiling. You see, I have this tuft of fur on my back, in front of my tail, which curls up. Pupp says I look like a duck; Mupp says it's cute.

One day, Mupp made a game of "pin the bling-bling on the husky." She fastened imitation diamond hair clamps to my head fur and duck tuft, and then affixed a matching necklace around my neck. Mupp called it a fashion show.

Well, as soon as I was all dressed up, I began to shake. I couldn't help myself. I did *not* care for items hanging on me. Hey, don't get me wrong. I love the bling, on Mupp. But when it's on me, it pulls on my fur and annoys me. I'm just not a jewelry parading dog. Mupp called me her Pretty Precious Princess, even without the bling.

After the fashion show, I decided to lie with Pupp and watch some howling wolves on television. They looked so peaceful singing their song. I didn't think they would mind if I join in. "Owwwooooooo," I sang. "Owwwoooooooo."

Mupp and Pupp giggled when I howled. Then, if I was following this correctly, I supposed they expected me to howl when they giggled. All right, I could do that. "Owwwoooooooo," I sang.

Pupp's mouth opened and he entered the song with me. I like singing, it perks me up, even if Pupp is a little off key.

Singing with the wolves was how I began to speak. When I was only a year old, I could say words like *out*, *why*, and *Mama*. Mupp thinks I'm adorable when I talk or howl.

All that singing made me wild and ready for a football game. I grabbed a toy, set it in Pupp's lap, put my chest on the floor, wiggled my rump in the air, and began to huff. Huff-huff, huff-huff. My huffing was greeted as an invitation. Pupp said, "Go long, Czarah, go long." He threw the ball; I scampered into the kitchen, caught the ball, brought it back to Pupp, and ran circles around him as he tried to catch me.

Wow, horseplay makes me thirsty, and with a big drink of water, I had to go potty. Mupp grabbed the camera and her coat and said, "Wait for me. The best pictures are taken outside in the sunshine."

Mupp is always taking my picture and entering contests. Recently, I won a photo contest for a dog and cat food corporation's calendar. I was in the centerfold, Miss June. I gladly accepted the prize of four cases of grain-free canned game: pheasant, buffalo, venison, and duck. All of the calendar profits went to animal shelters; so Mupp bought one for every member of the family. Afterwards, my nickname was changed to Pretty Princess Calendar Girl.

Anyway, it doesn't matter what time of year it is, I love the sunshine and the sounds of nature. The sun is good for my fur, keeping it shiny. There were so many things to smell, including the fresh cool air.

After some picture taking, Mupp returned to the house because it was too cold for her. Walking onward with Pupp, I was very surprised to see another dog treading beside me. Like a flash, I paused to socialize with it by saying, *"Hello there. Want to roughhouse?"* I pounced at it, and it pounced at me. I stood sideways in a pose, and it did too. When I walked away, it walked right beside me. I hopped like a bunny, and it hopped too. It appeared I had done this before. So I ran as fast as I could, and it ran beside me the whole time. This must have been my reflection showing off. But I hadn't seen her leave the house with us. I wondered how she got out.

Pupp began to laugh at me and said, "Czarah, are you prancing with your shadow? You are such a silly girl."

All right, I don't understand a reflection or a shadow. Pupp noticed my dumbfounded face and clarified, "In a reflection, you can see your face, your teeth, and your fur. In a shadow, you cannot see these things. Shadows are a dark likeness of something. Look at my hand." Pupp moved his hand just above the ground to show me his shadow.

This was great! If there were two of everything, I could entertain myself every day.

As we continued to walk and frolic with my new friend Shadow, cold white stuff began to fall from the sky. "Ah, look Czarah, it's snowing. You are going to like this!" Pupp said.

I am queen of the mountain.

I set out to snatch the snowflakes; however, bits kept landing on my nose and eyeballs. So, Pupp rounded up some snowballs to teach me how to catch. It was hard at first, but after a few snowy faces, I was catching every one.

Then he made a pretend squirrel hole in the snow and placed a treat in the bottom. "Dig, Czarah, dig, find the squirrel, find the treat, and burn up some of that energy," he said.

I knew there wasn't a squirrel in that hole. If there was, I would have been able to smell it. But, to satisfy Pupp, I dug for the yummy treat at the bottom.

I loved hunting for treats and kicking up my heels in the snow. It felt like I reached another goal with every new challenge. And, with each successful achievement, I climbed to the top of our neighbor's hill, announcing to the world with a howl that I was King of the Mountain!

Okay, so I was not King of the Mountain. I was Queen of the Mountain!

Pupp began chatting in a lively voice, "Someday, Czarah, I will guide my own sled dog team across the open country and *you* will be my lead dog. I will build a perfect sled; one that is mighty and will sail smoothly over blankets of snow, drifts and sleet."

"Me, a lead dog, wow! Now that's a recreation, a true adventure for me. I will even help you build the sled, Pupp. Where will we find more sled dogs? Oh, I can go on a quest by asking other dogs during our walks. You're my best friend, Pupp. I will do anything for you."

Sooner than I expected, along came a dog I could ask. *"Hi, I was wondering, would you care to join my sled dog team?"*

The Chihuahua replied with a high voice, *"I cannot pull a sled. I am much too little. I don't believe they make a pulling harness small enough."*

We strolled through the neighborhood park to watch the kids make snowmen, and along came another dog. *"Hello* there. You are a beautiful dog. Would you like to join my sled dog team?" I asked.

The poodle answered, *"I am sorry, I can't pull a sled. I am much too beautiful. I might mess up my fur or break one of my painted toenails."*

Every dog I asked said no. Gathering a team to pull Pupp's sled was harder than I thought. I didn't know if this was going to work for us. I decided I should have a talk with Mupp. Maybe she would have an idea.

When we arrived home from our walk, I ran straight for Mupp to tell her what happened. *"Mupp, it was so exciting, Mupp! I met other dogs and watched the kids in the park. They came over to pet me and scratch my ears. They thought I was a wolf, and there were so many new smells. I had a blast, Mupp! Can you take me somewhere to locate more dogs? We need a sled team for Pupp."*

"Wow, Pupp, Czarah is very excited about that walk in the park. Maybe we should find a dog show to visit. She might enjoy being around other Siberian huskies," Mupp said.

Pupp agreed and sat down to explore the Internet to find local dog shows. "Hey, Mupp, there is a Siberian husky Specialty Show this weekend in Pittsburgh, want to go?" Pupp asked.

"Good work, Pupp. We are going to our first dog show,"

Mupp said. "Czarah will love it!"

    Yes! This was perfect; she understood me. I hoped I would be able to find a sled team for Pupp at this dog show. Above all, it would be interesting. I might even learn something.

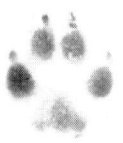

L.A. Adamson

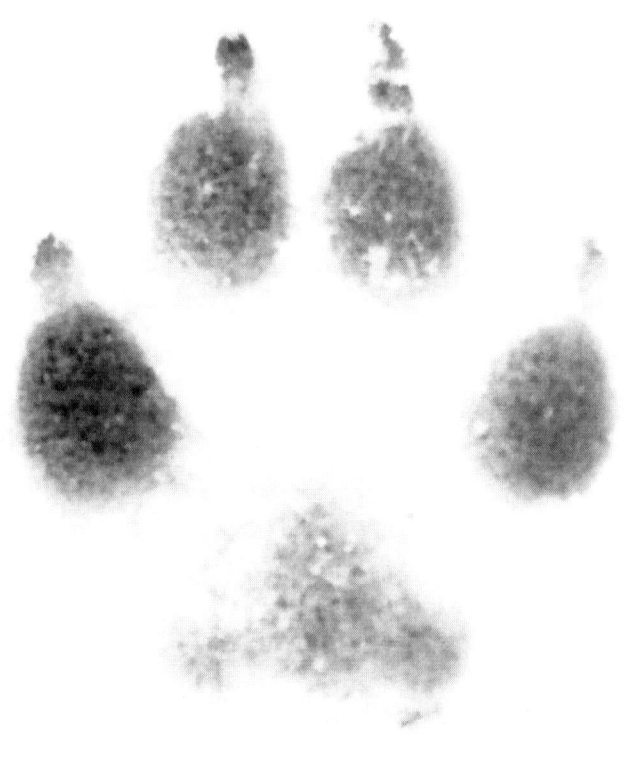

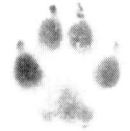

CHAPTER FOUR
MIRAGE

The weekend came upon us quickly. Mupp packed an overnight bag, just in case, while Pupp gave me a sparkling clean bath for the special event, then spoke with me during my brushing. "Czarah, you are growing up fast and have become a very pretty young lady. I expect you to act as such during this show. No galloping around and acting crazy like you do at home."

I focused on every word and said, *"I promise, Pupp. I will be a good girl, talk to all the dogs and find you a sled team. I won't let you down."*

The ride was long, taking two hours. On the way, I felt a little dizzy as I watched the trees go by and the lines on the road. When we reached the parking area, I saw huskies in cars, trucks, and campers. They looked just like me, except for a few that were different colors.

Mupp hooked the leash to my collar and said, "Czarah, come." Yes, this time I listened. I learned my lesson from the pet store episode.

Off we trotted across the parking lot into the arena. Siberian huskies were everywhere. They were passing by so quickly that I didn't have time to ask them about joining our sled team. All I could say was, *"Excuse me, would you..."* and they were gone.

We discovered our seats in the first row, right next to the show dogs. Wow, this was so exciting! They all looked extremely beautiful. Their fur was shiny, and they walked so tall and proud. Some were from other countries; I heard different languages spoken.

I saw reporters and cameras all around. I wondered if I would be on television. *"Oh no,"* I thought, *"there's no mirror at hand to see if my fur is in place."*

I noticed a big husky looking at me. I peered over my shoulder to see why he continued to glance my way, and I didn't see anything around me he could be looking at. *"All right,"* I thought, *"that is the sixth time he has gazed over here. Yes, I am counting."*

Mupp and Pupp took part in a chuckle, and when they chuckled, I howled. As I howled, everyone around us stared and laughed.

Then, Mupp said, "Czarah, I think you have an admirer. That husky is sweet on you."

"What do you mean, sweet on me?" I asked.

"That's the southern way of saying he likes you," Mupp said.

"Oh, he likes me. This is good; maybe he will help me find a sled team for Pupp," I said.

The announcer began to talk into the microphone. "Our first Siberian husky is an American, Canadian, and international champion. Please welcome Mirage to the ring."

Everyone clapped their hands and stood up to cheer, while I tried to rationalize why they called him "Mirage."

The dog and his handler trotted to the judge for inspection. The judge felt Mirage's fur from the top of his head to the tip of his tail. He also checked his vision and examined his teeth. Then he directed Mirage and his handler to jog to the end of the arena and back.

As he passed by me, his stare was hypnotic and his trot was as if he were floating across the floor. He had the most beautiful pale blue eyes I had ever seen. Suddenly I understood why they called him "Mirage." He was unreal!

He was persistent with his flirting by raising his brows up and down. Thank goodness for fur, considering my skin was blushing red. I couldn't help but stare back at him, he was so handsome.

After the show, Mupp and Pupp ventured to the grooming area to talk with handlers about how to show a dog. Mirage approached me with a big grin on his lip. *"Hello there, pretty girl. What's your name?"* he said.

Mirage

"Czarah Mae," I mumbled. He gave me a nudge with his nose as he escorted me away from the humans.

"*Join me in my grooming area. I have air conditioning,*" Mirage said.

We sat and talked while Mupp and Pupp continued to get information from the handlers. I asked, *"Why are you called Mirage?"*

He answered, *"I am a phantom, here today, then gone tomorrow."* He laughed. *"No, really, I am always on the road to another show. It's all I do. I travel all over the world."*

After a brief pause, he said, *"You have been here several hours, pretty lady. Would you like to drink some of my special vitamin water? It's cold and very good for you."*

"Sure, I am *somewhat thirsty,"* I told him.

After the drink, Mirage said, *"You have a little drop of water on your lip. Let me get that for you."* With a light touch of his tongue, he gently removed the drop, and contributed an affectionate nose rub.

"I like you, Czarah, and your elegant deer features," he said.

Just then Mupp called out, "Czarah, let's go."

"I feel confident we will see each other again," Mirage said.

"I look forward to meeting with you again," I responded. As I walked away, I turned my head back and whispered, "I like you too." I saw a twinkle in his eye as he winked.

When we reached the parking lot, Mupp said, "Pupp, do you see how Czarah is practically walking backwards? I think she is in love with that five-star pedigree, Mirage."

"Yes, I detect love in the air. He seems very nice," Pupp said.

"Oh no, I completely forgot to ask him if he knows any sled dogs. Pupp, can we go back?"

"The show was very entertaining and educational. There is another one tomorrow. Why don't we get a hotel, stay the night, have a nice dinner, and come back tomorrow?" Pupp asked.

"That sounds great!" Mupp said.

Yes, I would get a second chance to find a sled team.

"The dog show flyer advertises an impressive looking hotel across the street from the arena, with a glorious restaurant inside," Pupp said. He drove the truck to the hotel entrance and ran inside to ask if they accepted pets.

"Yes, sir, we do accept pets. Many of the show dogs stay here," the receptionist said.

"Wonderful! I would like a room for two, with one Siberian husky," Pupp said.

The receptionist asked, "Is it a show dog?"

"No," Pupp said. "We're only here to watch."

It was near dinner time; my tummy was beginning to growl as Mupp read the canine menu. "Chicken, beef, fish, or lamb and rice, are their choice meals, Czarah."

"I like chicken. Anything else does not agree with my tummy," I explained.

Mupp and Pupp changed into their fancy dinner clothes, and we strolled elegantly toward the restaurant, as my nose, by nature, led the way.

The hostess seated us next to a large window overlooking the indoor, heated pool. The exhibit of potted flowers and shrubs invited me to smell them. *"But not now,"* I thought, *"I'm hungry!"*

Mupp and Pupp ordered food I had never heard of and then ordered my favorite, chicken.

While we were waiting for our meals, I could see people gathering and cameras flashing on the other side of the restaurant. I wondered what was going on. When our server returned with yummy honey rolls as an appetizer, Pupp asked, "What's all the excitement over there?"

The server replied, "The famous Mirage, a bona fide champion Siberian husky, is with us this evening."

"Thank you," Pupp said.

"See, Czarah, your new friend is a true celebrity. You should talk more with him. Maybe he is acquainted with some sled dogs," Pupp said.

It wasn't long before our meals arrived. I couldn't wait much longer. I was starving! *"Mmmm, this is so good."*

After we ate, Mirage walked across the restaurant, nearing our table. He gave a gesture with his head to follow him, and then departed the room through a side door leading to the pool. I was interested in smelling the flowers and foliage anyway.

I pulled my ears back and surveyed Pupp's face, waiting for permission to walk by the pool and talk with Mirage about sled dogs. Pupp swallowed his food, nodded in approval and said, "Go ahead, Czarah."

When I arrived at the pool, Mirage was standing in the

Smelling the flowers.

shallow end, cooling his feet. I began with small talk on how much I loved the smell and beauty of flowers, as I inhaled the fragrance of a lily blossom.

"I too love the beauty of the outdoors. With regret, I am sensitive to the flowers. They make me sneeze," Mirage explained.

"Come for a swim. The water is nice," he continued.

As I slowly stepped into the cool pool water, the aroma of chlorine overwhelmed me. I swam for a moment, then darted onto the deck and asked Mirage if he wanted to go for a jaunt to dry off.

We raced around the hotel and took part in some tag, hide and seek, find the stick, and chase the squirrel. It was nice to have another dog to cut loose with.

After our amusement, we strolled back to the pool area and chatted for hours. I discovered we had much in common.

I told him about Pupp wanting his own sled dog team and asked him if he knew any dogs that would like to join our team.

He said, "I have the nose of a bloodhound. So, when I retire, I want to lead a sled dog search and rescue team. I know many canines that can't wait to be sled dogs. I will speak to them. Nevertheless, you will have your team in a few months."

He walked me to the hotel room, and I thanked him kindly for a wonderful evening with a kiss on his cheek. I scratched at the door, and Pupp let me in.

Excited that we would be getting a sled team, I couldn't wait to tell Pupp. But Pupp was tired and whispered, "Czarah, it's three o'clock in the morning. You're going to awake sleeping people next door. Can we talk about this later?"

Disappointed, I curled up in my bed and had happy thoughts about hustling the sled team as a lead dog. I was not

Sled dog training.

worried about rest. I could sleep during the long drive to the homestead.

After the second dog show, on our way home, Pupp talked with Mupp about getting parts for the sled and how he was going to train me as his lead dog. He rehearsed the sled commands and discussed building a sled on which he would be able to alternate wheels with skis—wheels for seasons without snow, skis for seasons with snow. It was a bit confusing to me.

Here are the commands we used in training:
~ Hike!: Mush or run
~ Kissing sound: Faster
~ Gee!: Right turn
~ Haw!: Left turn
~ Easy!: Slow
~ Whoa!: Stop
~ On by!: Keep going

This seems like a lot to remember. But after you do it a few times, it gets easier.

Sled dog training requires much exercise. My muscle tone was ideal for a husky celebrating her second birthday. I was growing with leaps and bounds, and I was now considered a full grown husky.

At that time we had been pull training with a long rope, like tug o' war. I was such a good puller; Pupp praised me with treats, and by telling me I was such a good girl.

Before long, Pupp was almost done building the sled, and I was about to become a genuine sled dog.

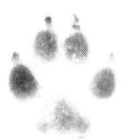

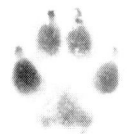

CHAPTER FIVE
COW BELLY GIRL

After a month of training, Mupp declared, "Czarah is getting bigger every day. Maybe I shouldn't give her cupcakes on her birthday. She's becoming a chubby little girl."

"Yes, I agree," Pupp replied. "Too chubby. I've read if the belly is swollen on a dog, it may have worms."

"Worms? Gross—that is disgusting!" said Mupp. "I will call right now for a veterinary appointment and talk to them about a worm preventative."

"Worms? I don't have worms! Chubby! I am not chubby. I am physically fit from all this training. Then again, maybe I shouldn't have eaten that last cupcake."

"They have an opening to see her at 5:00 this afternoon," Mupp told Pupp. "Just the thought of worms inside of our precious princess sickens me."

Before long, I was at the vet's office, prancing around to get attention from the technicians. They tried to be nice and gave me chalky flavored dog treats. I spit them on the floor, hoping that someday they would get some tasty treats in there. (Eventually they did.)

The technician entered the room and said, "This is a cotton swab to get a sample to check for worms. We place the sample between two slides and inspect it under a microscope for parasites. This will take about five minutes, and then the veterinarian will be in to talk with you."

During those five minutes, I decided to check the exam room thoroughly. There were some terrible smells in here, too many to discuss. I mean—the room looked clean. But dogs have a proven gift of scent, compared to humans. We can smell things long after all the cleaning.

When the veterinarian opened the exam room door, I had just sprung to the countertop for further investigating. Bad timing—that was *not* a good idea. As my feet landed on the slippery counter, it was as though I had no brakes at all. The tissues, cotton balls, exam gloves, and hand washing soap sailed into the air and onto the floor. The whole plight was quite embarrassing. Mupp and Pupp scrambled to pick up everything, as they apologized for my behavior.

I sat peacefully as the veterinarian translated the test findings. "There is no sign of worms, or parasites of any kind. I suggest we do an ultrasound on her belly to see what the trouble is."

"Sure, that sounds like a good idea," Mupp told the doctor.

We embarked into an area with surgical equipment and a much larger table that was lowered to the floor. I stepped up and lay on the table as they raised it about three feet. I was scared, but Mupp held my paws the entire time, while the doctor gave a reason for all she was doing.

The doctor was using an ultrasound wand; it had a magic eye on the end to survey the inside of my stomach. When the doctor moved the wand along my belly, it felt like a massage. Then the results were displayed on a monitor screen.

"Well now, here is your trouble," the doctor said. "You will be having puppies."

"*What*? Puppies! Are you sure?" Mupp and Pupp asked.

"Oh yes, I'm sure. I counted three, but there may be more hidden," the doctor said.

"Czarah Mae! What have you done?" Pupp asked.

"*What! I didn't do anything! What's going on?*"

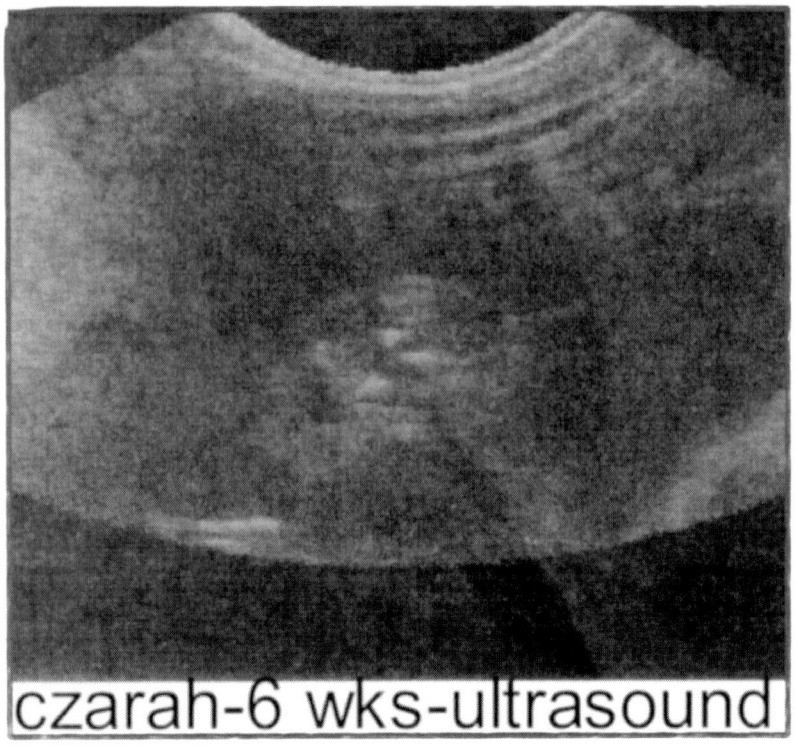

The doctor gave me chewable peanut butter flavored prenatal vitamins that I must eat twice daily and sent us home with information to read.

"Hmmm, puppies—I don't know if this is a good thing or a bad thing. I know nothing about having puppies," Pupp said.

On our way home, Mupp made a quick stop at the grocery store and bought a couple of chicken soup packs, made of chicken meat and fat scraps. Then, she explained puppies to us and how I needed to exercise and eat a balanced diet, so they would be born healthy and strong.

"Thoroughly cooked chicken soup packs are Czarah's treat food from now on. There are no additives or preservatives like the store brand treats on the shelf, and her dog food will be all natural, or organic. When you feed your dog or puppies healthy food, they will grow up to be healthy, which prevents future veterinary bills," Mupp said.

In the meantime, I needed to continue light activities, such as everyday lifting of my toys, tug o' war with my bee-wow-wow (Mupp and Pupp call it a rope), and jogs around the neighborhood, the park, and to the downtown stores.

I had a month to go before motherhood, carrying my puppies for a total of sixty-three days. That's not very long, just over two months. Becoming a mother is a huge commitment. I was sure I could do this; I was eager to be a wonderful mom to my babies.

Pupp was a bit nervous about the puppies coming. He wanted every little thing to be perfect for me. He did a lot of reading about puppies and announced that it was time to build a birthing box in my bedroom. He said, "We need to keep the babies secure, so they don't get into something that may hurt them. I will use two-by-eight size lumber from my sled. Don't worry, Czarah; the lumber can easily be replaced."

Meanwhile, I was getting bigger and bigger every day and

Lifting a toy for exercise.

couldn't seem to get comfortable when I lay down. I walked in circles and fluffed the soft blankets that Grandma made for me into a pile. But it still felt like I was sleeping on rocks.

Then a strange thing happened. I had a driving desire to clean and cuddle five of my toys hourly, as if they were my real babies. Therefore, I believed there would be five puppies. It must have been instinct.

Pupp just came home from work. *"If I lie on my back,"* I thought, *"maybe he'll rub my belly for me."*

"Oh look, it's cow-belly girl. Awe, does my big cow-belly girl need a tummy rub?" Pupp laughed.

"Ah, thank you, Pupp. I love you!"

As Pupp rubbed my belly, he felt the puppies move. "Oh my goodness, Mupp, come feel the puppies—they're doing cartwheels," he said.

They sat with smiles on their faces as their hands rested on my tummy. Then they took guesses about the puppies I was carrying: how many boys, how many girls, their eye colors, and their fur colors. They predicted that all the puppies would be black and white, and half of them would have blue eyes. Hmmm, I wondered how accurate they were.

All those mini cartwheels made me have to potty. I struggled to stand up, as my big belly was in the way of everything. I shuffled to the door; Mupp followed and hooked the leash to my collar. It was very cold out, and the ground was covered with snow, as I waddled all over the yard, sniffing for the perfect spot.

Suddenly, Mupp called out, "Czarah, look! There's a comet shooting across the sky."

I gazed at the glittering white ray of light as it gracefully crossed the horizon. It was breathtaking.

At the same time, I was struck with a sharp pain in my tummy. "Owwwoooooo," I howled at the comet. My legs become weak, as I descended to the soft snow that gently accepted me. I tried to relax in thought of my puppies, while I watched the frosty smoke from my breath just above the frozen fluff.

Then, I become aware of an angelic energy, Anevay my great-grandmother, respectfully whispering a message to me:

One dawn to one dusk, a gift of speech unites. Gain insight swiftly from protectors alike. One dawn to one dusk, on a voyage to seek. Trust keen insight, for you shall no longer speak.

"Pupp, come quickly," Mupp cried. "Something's wrong with Czarah. She let out a howl and collapsed to the ground. I hope our girl is all right."

As Pupp carried me indoors, I tried to communicate with Anevay. *"I've missed you. Thank you for visiting me. I love you."* But she was gone.

My tummy hurt—and my back, and my legs, and my hips. I certainly felt my puppies were about to be born. I promptly grabbed my blanket with one swipe of my toenails and began to push for the first puppy.

Concerned, Mupp and Pupp stayed by my side, helping any way they could. Every five minutes, they offered me cold water.

"It's about to happen—I have never seen puppies born before. This is truly amazing!" Pupp said.

I let out a yelp and Pupp turned white as a sheet. Mupp helped with the delivery and fanned Pupp with a notebook to prevent him from passing out. "Are you all right?" Mupp asked him.

"Our firstborn is a black and white boy," Mupp said.

"Wow, uh, he's so cute. You know, suddenly I don't feel so good," Pupp said.

"I can't care for both of you at the same time, so concentrate on taking care of Czarah," Mupp said.

So, without looking at the birthing area, Pupp gave me cold water and dabbed my head with a chilled washcloth, while Mupp continued to help with the deliveries and take photographs.

"Puppy number two is a black and white boy," Mupp said. "Puppy number three is a red and white girl. There goes our guesswork for all black and whites," Mupp continued.

I relaxed for a while, because I knew there were more to bring forth, but Mupp and Pupp thought I was done and prepared themselves for bed. I wrestled with my blanket, trying to tell them I was not finished. When Mupp saw this, she felt my belly. "Hey, Pupp, she's not done—I feel another puppy," she said.

So we waited, and waited, and waited. Morning came; I was feeling no pain, and still no puppy. Mupp called the

A loving nap.

veterinary office, concerned, and relying on their help. "They say to bring her in right away," Mupp declared.

The doctor checked me thoroughly and agreed there was one more puppy to be born. She gave me a shot in the rump to bring about labor and then sent us home.

Back home, Mupp and Pupp took turns gently rubbing my belly, hoping to move the puppy into the birthing position. It helped; two hours later another boy was born. This fellow was red and white, and gigantic. He was twice the size of the others.

Mupp and Pupp watched in wonder as I adjusted my blanket for the unforeseen fifth puppy. "I thought she was done. I can't believe Czarah collected and cared for five of her playthings, with the insight she was carrying five babies," Pupp said. "That's amazing!"

A few minutes later, Mupp said, "It's another black and white boy. This one's a giant too. We have four boys and one girl, three black and white, two red and white. Wow, these last two are so big!"

Mupp felt my belly to make sure I was not hiding any more. "Her belly is soft. No more hidden puppies," Mupp said.

Kissing my newborn baby.

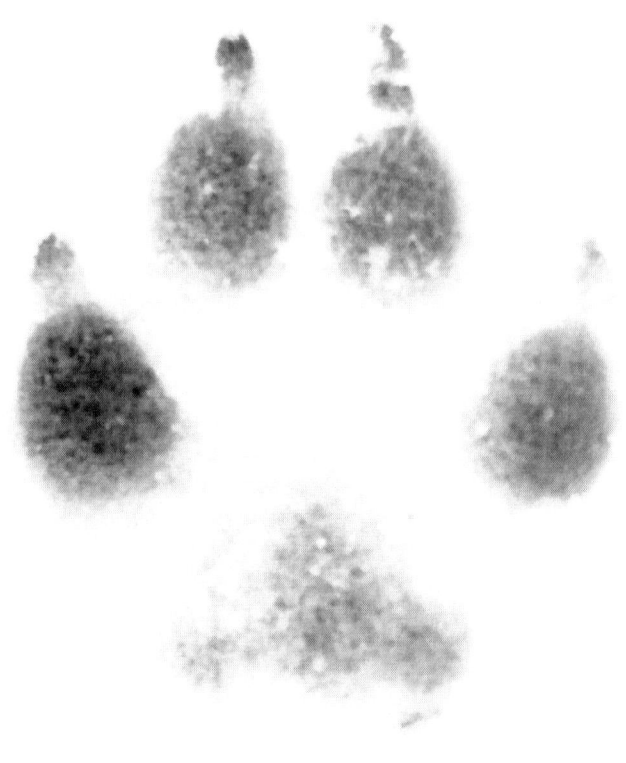

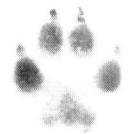

CHAPTER SIX
THE BIG MOVE

I treasured my babies. They were so small and helpless, crawling about with heads that bobbed up and down. As we watched their personalities unfold during their bonding as siblings, we considered Native American names for each.

Mupp and Pupp were so delighted about the puppies; they took a new picture every three minutes. After a while, the camera flash hurt my eyes.

Next, I heard a knock at the door. *"Perfect timing,"* I thought. *"If I see one more camera flash, I'm going to hide my head under my pillow. It's Grandma!"* I was eager to see my Grandma. I showed her my love and affection by huffing in her face and giving her a little socket love. *"Oh no, she brought her camera."*

Camera flashes hurt my eyes.

Mupp, Pupp, Grandma and I sat for the longest time watching fuzzy little sleeping bodies twitch and their tiny paws wiggle up and down. They made squeaky noises, grunted out loud and took their turns with puppy-cups. That's what Mupp called their hiccups. The big red one was steadfast on the milk breast, jerking his head back, trying to drain every last drop.

"In two or three weeks their peepers will open. Their eye color can be brown, blue or amber," Mupp said.

I was constantly caring for my babies. They were always hungry, wanting milk, crying because they couldn't find the milk, in need of a good spit bath, and desiring hugs and kisses. They were so precious to me. *"When they're ready,"* I thought, *"I will teach them everything I know, including all the things Mupp and Pupp taught me. For instance: sled dog training, rules of the house, all the tricks I know—Sled dog training! Oh my goodness, I found our sled dog team! Pupp, this is wonderful, we finally have our team."*

Sleeping babies.

I had to get Pupp's attention. How would I tell him? What should I do? Pupp detected my strange behavior and said, "Czarah, what's wrong with you?"

"Hold everything, I have an idea." Instantly, I ran to my harness. I picked it up with my teeth, carried it to the birthing box, and set it on the babies.

Pupp said, "No, Czarah. You'll hurt the babies. They can't wear a harness and go outside."

He picked the harness off the babies and attempted to put it on me, assuming I wanted to go out. I dodged the head opening, left, and then right. "Be still, Czarah," Pupp said. I latched onto the harness with my teeth, pulled it from Pupp's hands, and lightly laid it over the babies again. "No, Czarah," Pupp said.

"Now what can I do? Wait, I have another idea." I went into the bathroom, clutched Pupp's sled dog book in my mouth, and transported it to my offspring. Then I latched onto the harness and laid it on the book.

Pupp followed along this time and let out a joyful cry. "Sled dog team! This is wonderful news, Czarah Mae. Good girl, you are so smart." Pupp described to Mupp everything that just happened and revealed his need of the remaining sled materials.

After discussing the entire situation of adding five more Siberian huskies to our small family and training them for sled dog recreations, they both agreed that we needed a bigger house. So Pupp went shopping for sled materials, while Mupp went shopping for a bigger house.

The next several months went by fast. Mupp and Pupp dedicated all their spare time to training and maintaining a normal routine. Before long, all the babies knew what to do and exactly what time to do it. They were so smart and talented.

As time went by, I remembered exactly what my mother and great-grandmother taught me, and I used that knowledge to help Mupp and Pupp teach my babies excellent Siberian husky temperament skills. All of them possessed great spirits, except for the female, who was fighting for the alpha position. She was a sassy little terror who gave me a heap of trouble, battling her brothers with growls and disobedience. There's simply one alpha in this family and that's me—and of course, Mupp. I hoped that this female would learn quickly. We had a few disputes, but after a while she realized her position in the pack.

In spite of everything, Mupp was persistent with the weekly house seeking and returned one day carrying moving boxes, convinced she had clearly found a winner. When Pupp arrived home from work, she commented on the features and said, "It's located just across town and has three bedrooms, two bathrooms, new carpeting, new kitchen appliances, and new windows. It's recently painted, inside and out. And I love the exterior—they've recently landscaped with shade trees and shrubs."

They left for a few hours to inspect the house from top to bottom. Upon returning, Mupp said, "Czarah Mae, we found a new house, and it's perfect! We made an offer. If the owner places a fence around the backyard for you and the babies, we will buy it."

Meanwhile, the real estate agent called the owner about the fence and he agreed. Excitement filled the air, with wagging tails suggesting we would all be much happier in this new house. Soon after, a fence company began to excavate the sloped yard and drill holes for the posts. It only took a few days, and the six-foot, white privacy fence was complete.

The closing on the house was arranged for a week later, October thirty-first, Halloween day. Mupp and Pupp still found time to dress us in costumes. I was a princess, of course. The puppies were dressed as a bear, a hula girl, a bee, a clown, and a frog. For the last time, I sat on that front porch with my puppies while candy was handed out. All the neighborhood kids loved us in our costumes, and we loved them, except for their sticky hands on the top of our heads.

The day after the house closing, Mupp and Pupp were packed and prepared for the move. They were also looking forward to releasing me and the babies to roam freely in the yard without a leash or tie out. Mupp gently loaded us into their SUV truck, whereas Pupp drove the moving truck.

When we arrived, Mupp was excited for me as she delivered me to the doggy door. Of course, I had no idea what it was, so I just stood there and looked at it while Mupp told me to go through. She could see I was nervous about entering a place I had never been before, so, head first, Mupp crawled through the door, showing me how it was done. I understood and copied her by pushing the long plastic flap with my head, meeting her on the other side.

Before Mupp collected the babies from the truck, we walked throughout the yard until I became comfortable with my new surroundings.

I wandered while Mupp slipped away to collect the babies. When she reached the truck, she captured one of the puppies completely satisfied whilst eating a seatbelt as an afternoon snack. "Oh no," Mupp said. "Bad boy!" she told him. His puppy teeth were so sharp that it looked as though someone had cut it with a pair of scissors.

His ears went back and his head dropped down, saying he was sorry. "That's a really sad face, baby. I can't stay mad at a face like that. I never should have left you alone," Mupp said with a grin.

One by one, Mupp placed the babies next to me in the grass. After wandering around, we entered the doggy door from the outside and ran down the stairs to a finished basement and found our bedding and belongings.

Princess costume.

We scoped out the area and located a box fan hanging from the ceiling. It tilted toward the floor for comfort. We had new, raised double feeders—one bowl for water, the other for chow-chow. Opposite our beds, on a concrete platform, was an electric fireplace heater to take the chill out of the air during the upcoming winter. Located on a high wooden shelf was our bag of chow-chow and a small television for entertainment. We had all the comforts of life in this new home.

Telling my babies a story.

L.A. Adamson

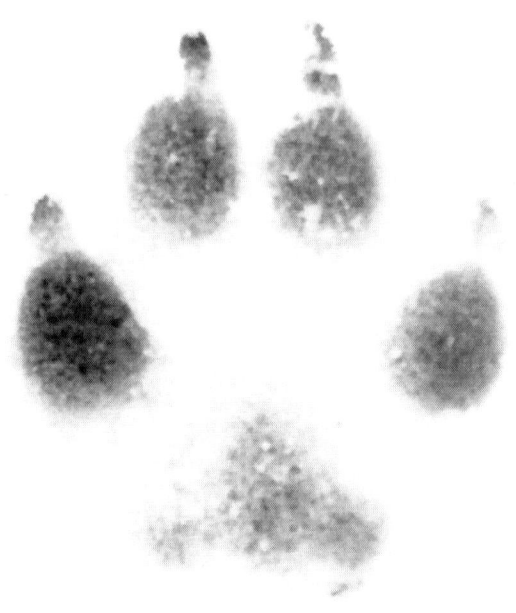

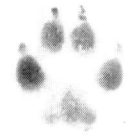

CHAPTER SEVEN
UNIQUE NAMES

A few weeks later and with lots of help from Grandma, unpacking was almost complete. We could relax and enjoy our beautiful home and concentrate on our family.

All along, Pupp was building his sled and thinking of great husky names. He decided to name the first born Indy, as a result of his fearless investigating, equal to that of Indiana Jones. He was a friendly, bi-eyed boy with one blue eye and one brown. We nicknamed him: Great Big Tiger and Lover boy.

Indy loved his Pupp and followed him in every direction. He was the first to crawl out of the birthing box, over and over again, searching for Pupp while exploring every little thing in a calm, cool manner.

For several weeks Mupp dealt with a mystery; someone kept stealing the caps off the laundry soap bottles. There was never any evidence. They just disappeared—until Mupp heard one of the puppies sneezing, repeatedly. She rushed downstairs to find that this very independent boy had accomplished an impossible task by stacking empty moving

Caught on the laundry table.

boxes to scale onto the laundry table. There sat Indy, sneezing his head off and caught with a cap between his front paws. Like me, he loved removing all caps. Mupp was truly pleased he didn't notice the bleach bottle.

As much as Indy loved the laundry caps, he was actually allergic to the strong smell of detergent and fabric softener. Mupp had to downgrade her detergent and stop using fabric softener in our blankets due to Indy's sneezing. I suppose he takes after his dad with allergies.

A work friend of Pupp's named the second born Neko, meaning Cat, considering his cat-like reflexes and the way he pawed at his playthings. Neko devoted himself to acting as night watchman, resting under the stars on a flat-top dog house that Pupp built with spare wood from the sled. He listened for and captured the evening moles in the yard and placed them in the exact spot every time, on the limestone rocks under the kitchen window.

When Mupp opened the kitchen blinds in the morning, the first vision of the day was a dead mole spread out on the rocks, baking in the sun. Yuck! Neko merely wanted Mupp to be proud of his accomplishment, and she was, saying thank you every time. We nicknamed him: Ne-ko-la, Neko Talarico, Kola, Wolfy, and Hoarder.

Neko's first sign of communication began with a boo-boo on his foot. Through his charcoal black eyes, he shyly peeked at Mupp and conveyed his urgency with such a creepy, profoundly low-toned grumble, it captured Mupp's attention the first time she heard it.

Apparently, he stepped on a pine needle and needed to get her attention, and did so by speaking the word, "Home," with his eerie, shallow tone. Clearly, he didn't know how to say boo-boo. Yes, Neko said his first word and then lifted his paw to show that he required her assistance.

When Mupp took his paw in hand, she felt the pine needle and quickly removed it. To prevent infection, she rubbed Neosporin™, an excellent antibiotic ointment, on the affected area. Later she started calling the product "Neko-sporin," because of Neko's tendency to get so many boo-boos.

Neko's favorite thing to do was to choose a ball, chase it and not allow anyone else to get near it. He bared his teeth to scare his siblings by telling them he was sincere about keeping the ball. Mupp and Pupp called this his "Neko smile."

No, Neko did not share. Therefore, he was often left alone to play, while the others had fun together, until he fell asleep.

Neko had a tough time staying awake and often fell asleep

sitting up. Mupp and Pupp said he had "Neko-lepsy." What they really meant was narcolepsy, which is a sleep disorder. It meant Neko had a severe urge to sleep at the wrong times, and as soon as he was dozing, someone stole his ball. He always woke without his prize possession, and then went on a rampage to find it.

Playing in the snow for the first time.

Also, Neko was not partial to take notice when his name was called. After watching a cough drop commercial on television, Mupp had an idea and beckoned, "Neeee-ko-laaaaaa." He bustled so quickly to Mupp, his body couldn't keep up with his feet. This was the only way he would come when called.

Then there was Samarah Nayele. Her name means "guarded by God through the forest." This title was given to her with hopes that she would someday turn out to be a little angel, instead of a pint size terror that lets out a screech at the top of her lungs for no reason at all. She was addressed as Sam, or Sami when well-behaved. We nicknamed her: Supermodel, Honey Badger, Pretty-Pretty Sami, and Wild thing.

This puppy continued to push me for the Alpha position. Mupp said as soon as Samarah was old enough, we would both be spayed. Supposedly, this would ease her bossiness and prevent needless pregnancies.

Sami adored water in the kiddy pool and repeatedly plunged nose first to wet the other puppies and squirm about like a duck. Yet during a bath, she literally climbed the shower walls crying to get out.

Sam believed she was a supermodel, the most beautiful dog in the world, holding her head high and generally lying in a pose with her front arms crossed. Then she would flash her attractive, amber eyes with that blank supermodel look on her face. But, oddly enough, when it was raining, she would dig holes in the dirt, and then delve into the muddy cavities with all fours. She was so filthy you couldn't make out her hair color.

Samarah's supermodel pose.

She was also a professional locksmith, opening almost any door in the house with a slap of her paw. She had a special interest in the deadbolts. Sometimes, Mupp and Pupp were quite surprised to find us wandering throughout the house when neither of them had let us upstairs.

Otherwise, she maintained her brothers with a daily spit bath, especially the two fuzzy mammoths who couldn't reach certain areas because they were too bulky to stretch that far.

When Sami was bored, she often occupied herself by chewing and burrowing her head through the rugs and blankets, so she could wear them like a skirt and flaunt her beauty. Or, she chose to bolt around the furniture so fast you could imagine she was a car on a racetrack.

Mupp labeled the fourth born, Cheveyo Meoquanee. He was called Chevy for short. He reminded us of a big Chevy truck with endless speed and massive pulling ability.

Everything about Chevy was big, including his hefty eating. We nicknamed him: Chev-Chev, Handsome, Tiny Little Puppy, and Big Brown Bear.

Cheveyo Meoquanee is Native American for "ghost warrior wears red." Sometimes he acted like a ghost, lurking about, thieving playthings and hiding them in his cubbyhole, and when he was lying in the sun, his copper color turned a light red.

Chevy was quite affectionate; he snuggled and rolled his head on anyone who smelled of perfume or fabric softener sheets, in addition to fuzzy slippers and clean blankets.

During our former Halloween dress up, his outfit of choice had been a bear costume. Chevy's ears wouldn't stand up straight like the other huskies, so he believed he was a big brown bear trapped in a tiny puppy's body. When bustling about, his oversize frame would leap into the air and plunge onto Mupp's or Pupp's settled lap. When he was airborne, he really looked like a big bear coming at you.

Chevy had the nose of a bloodhound. Playing hide and seek with him was a blast. He found every grain of popcorn that Mupp or Pupp concealed between and under the couch cushions. If someone lost a treat or piece of food under the furniture, stove, or refrigerator, Chevy knew precisely where it was.

Pupp had a stack of four tires he couldn't seem to get rid of, so he glued them together and threw a bunch of treats inside. Then he threw toys inside to cover up the treats; Chevy would dive to the bottom and find the dainty morsels. All you could see was a wagging tail at the top tire rim. But if

Chevy and Indy in their cubbyhole.

a musical show appeared on television, he would walk away from treat searching to watch it. Musicals consumed him.

Chevy enjoyed a good game of kickball with his family. Then afterwards, he would stick his butt in the air with his front legs on the ground, begging for Indy to chase his long fluffy tail, which they truly believed was nothing but a plaything.

Indy loved chasing his brother, and Chevy loved running from Indy. These two spent the most time together; they were best friends and shared many things. Just like me, they gathered snippets of this and that to hide in Chevy's cubbyhole.

Chevy was famous for plopping his rear end in the chow-chow bowl, then declaring, *"No one wants this chow-chow my butt's in, right? So I can eat it all, right?"* That's why we each received raised double feeders in our new house. They were too high for Chevy to put his rump into.

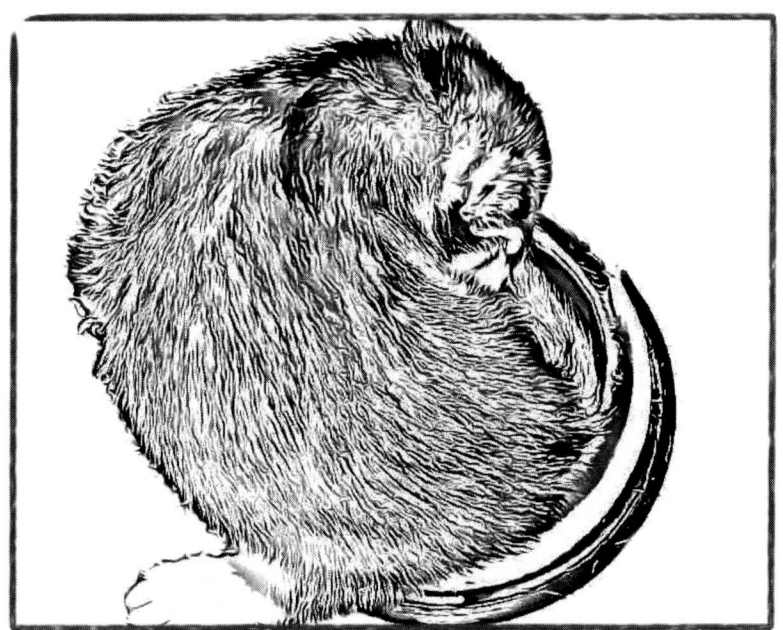

Claiming the chow-chow.

He paraded around with a whale of a smile, loving the camera and posing for the next picture with his adorable amber eyes. His favorite foods were spaghetti or potatoes and gravy, and he did not like bread or fruit.

Chevy's whale of a smile.

Mupp awarded the last big puppy born with the name, Tikaani Atka. This too is Native American, meaning "wolf guardian spirit." Since he was such a large boy with piercing ice blue eyes, she thought his name should be majestic. We nicknamed him: Kaan, King Kaan, Stinky, Dusty, and Pigpen.

Tikaani had the best attitude of them all. He was a wonderful, kind, loving, jumping, playful, freckle-face boy that had no sense of how massive he really was. He didn't pay attention to anything around him and walked or bounced backwards into walls, plants and people.

Without a doubt, King Kaan was the omega in the pack. When it got a little rough during playtime, Kaan was the first to lie down on his back and turn on the scream machine.

Kaan and Chevy had a lot in common with their sympathetic temperaments. Both used a very sad "nobody ever feeds me" face to get what they wanted. It worked every time!

Tikaani never got mad, but one day, he became very upset with Neko. When Kaan turned his head to look at someone, Neko ate his chow-chow. In just two gulps, it was gone. Just then, Neko was dubbed with a new name when Kaan yelled out, *"Oh you, jigger-a-doo!"* Mupp and Pupp had no idea what that meant, but I did. It means *"Oh you, terrible dog!"*

Soon winter was upon us. During the first snow Kaan became so excited, he came running inside, seriously expressing himself again. In a high pitched voice he howled, "Rooooo, rooooo!" So, every time it snowed, Mupp and Pupp would say, "Kaan, it's rooing outside." It was so sweet the way we conformed Mupp and Pupp to our husky way of life. They spoke our words and often with some success, we tried to speak theirs.

Tikaani was the pigpen of all huskies. After the snow melted, he took pride in rolling throughout the backyard mud. Then he would come into the house and rub against everyone, or shake the mud onto his family members. He clothed himself in dirt so much that when he was petted, dust flew off of him. He was promptly bathed after each episode and then refused to be brushed. He swore Mupp and Pupp were pulling his hair out and cried for them to put it back.

Rooooo, it's snowing outside.

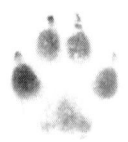

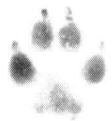

CHAPTER EIGHT
PREPARING FOR THE RACE

Mupp and Pupp had been training with the babies and were finding it quite difficult to educate and organize five absentminded puppies that were not about to obey one little command. So they arranged to take Indy and Chevy to behavioral classes. Armed with knowledge and skills from obedience school, Mupp and Pupp planned to train the other babies.

Kindergarten turned out to be interesting for Indy. Three different instructors praised him, saying, "There's something about Indy," while Chevy went into hiding under Mupp's chair during the entire six-week course.

Therefore, a six-week session of the beginner's class was highly recommended by the teacher. Chevy did much better this time. With Indy's help, he achieved a five-point

Indy's graduation.

Chevy's graduation.

lead, surpassing Indy upon completion of their graduation test. Mupp was so delighted; she cooked steaks and baked potatoes for all of us. The siblings were very proud of their brothers; they looked up to them as a result of their achievements and copied every little thing they did. This made sled dog workouts much easier on Mupp and Pupp.

They had used praise, understanding, determination, and lots of affection to prime the babies (now referred to as "kids") for the twenty-four-hour Great Pennsylvania Sled Dog Race, only a month away. With plenty of sled dog training behind us, the kids were excited that their first Christmas was approaching.

During our downtime, Mupp had begun a daily routine of inviting each of us to perform a trick or a part of our training exercise for a morning cookie. Chevy would take it a bit further and pretend it was a hot, jumping cookie. He pawed, pounced, and slapped that cookie until it cooled off and stopped jumping before he began to nibble on it.

The entertainment continued with Chevy the comedian as he suddenly refused to eat his daily "jumping cookie" until all the other kids were done with theirs, and then Mupp had to break it into four pieces and toss them, one by one, in the air to be caught, spit out and chased. This was one strange dog!

Another common episode was the everyday assault of the octa-mop, a tangle of material used to mop the floors. Mupp named it octa-mop because of the eight surviving strands left hanging. The kids liked to slap, paw, kick, bite, and sit on it, trying to make the octa-mop surrender. But it lived on, absorbing accidental puddles of pee several times a day.

Adding to our adventures, Pupp and Indy had an unexpected, frightening incident with a snowplow one evening. It appeared the plow driver did not see the two on the edge of the road, walking up a hill. The snow was piled at least four feet high, and there was no place for them to escape the roadway. Pupp told us that Indy dug into the ice and snow with his nails and pulled Pupp to safety, just as the plow hurdled past, missing them by inches. So Mupp made steaks again, to celebrate Indy's bravery.

Christmas was drawing near, so Mupp and Pupp went tree shopping. An hour later, they returned with a beautiful, green tree, perfect for the foyer area. Then they rummaged through the attic boxes for lights and ornaments to hang, including handmade stockings for all of us. Mupp handcrafted them with each of our names written in glitter. As she hung the stockings over the living room archway, she announced the names in pack order: Czarah, Indy, Chevy, Samarah, Neko, and Tikaani.

While decorating the tree, Mupp noticed Neko staring at his stocking. She told him, "You can't have it until Christmas morning." Hours went by, and he continued to stare and periodically cry for his stocking, until he fell asleep sitting up. At that time, Pupp carried him to bed.

On Christmas morning, the first gifts handed out were from the stockings. This made Neko a very happy boy. Mupp showed the kids how to open their Christmas presents. To get them started, she helped with a tear here and a rip there.

After the first present was open, they had no trouble performing the task themselves. Except for Chevy—he had no interest in opening anything and abruptly disappeared. We looked everywhere, until we heard Mupp giggle and ask, "Chevy, why are you hiding in the basement?"

He gave her a look as if to say, *"I'm not hiding. I'm just down here."*

Well, a few minutes later, Chevy came back to the Christmas celebration of toys and gourmet foods. Pupp had the video camera on and caught him sneaking away to the basement with one of the presents. He kept doing it, again, and again, and again. Opened and unopened presents, he was stealing them all one by one and hiding them under his blanket.

So Mupp collected the hidden treasures and told Chevy, "No!" She explained that taking things that don't belong to you is called stealing and it's not nice. He gave her a kiss on the cheek and went back upstairs to open presents with the others. We had lots of fun playing with our new toys, and the kids continued to teach Neko about sharing, but he still refused.

The month of December flew by. Before we realized it, we were preparing for the race to start as Pupp attached our harnesses and race equipment. We loved the snow, and during this time the sky was dropping snowflakes the size of quarters; this could make it challenging for Pupp to see signs and stay on the trail.

Pupp hooked us up two by two. In the front were Indy and I as the lead dogs. Lead dogs must have excellent communication with their sled team driver. Then Neko and Chevy were in the middle as the swing dogs, which are interchangeable, and Kaan and Sami were in the back as the wheel dogs. They had the most muscle and strength for pulling.

This was the day Pupp and I had waited for our whole lives, and I could tell he was very nervous. He knelt down next to me with concern on his face and a sparkle in his eyes, so I gave him some socket love, hoping to lighten his concerns, and as usual it worked. He laughed and told me he loved me. I gave him my *"Don't worry, I have this under control,"* look. He gave me a big hug and kiss, and told me he trusted me completely. This was great assurance.

Then, he continued with a nice little speech for all of us. "I have all the confidence in the world that we can win this race. But, remember what is most important—the safety and health of our family and friends. A race is just a race, but our family and friends are everything! Ready? Let's do this!"

We accepted Pupp's speech with friendly howls and barks as he triple checked the harnesses, sled, supplies, and all of us kids. He stood proud on the footboards of the sled, until the air horn sounded. At that point, Pupp said, "Mush!" and then he blew Mupp a kiss.

We hurried off in perfect form to reach our course at a steady speed. Unfortunately, we were only gone ten minutes and Pupp had to stop because something was wrong with Sami. She kept jerking her head back and forth, coughing and sneezing.

When Pupp approached Sami to investigate, Chevy let out a great big, stinky gas ball. Sami displayed her acting abilities with more coughs and sneezing, before crying for Pupp to do something.

Therefore, he had to unhook Chevy from the harness, attach him to the leash, and walk him into the woods to take care of his business. Apparently, Chevy was too nervous to go number two that morning.

Well, that wasn't a quick fix. Before Chevy could do his business, it was necessary to find the right spot. And if anyone was looking at him, he wouldn't go.

Sledding

After a good five minutes or so, he finally accomplished his task. To satisfy Sami, Pupp switched Chevy and Kaan on the gangline—this is a line that connects to the sled and all the dogs. This put Chevy in the rear, just in case he got gassy again.

"Mush! Off we go," said Pupp. A few hours went by, and

we were abruptly hit with another terrible odor. "It's a skunk!" Pupp shouted. "It's on the trail!" To avoid the little stinker, the sled went into a skid, broke away from the trail at a high speed, bounced off a tree, and damaged one of the runners. Neko defended his family by giving that skunk his Neko smile. I was so mad; I stood there growling with my hair straight up on my back. Good thing I was attached to the gangline or that critter would have been my afternoon snack. Then again, maybe that wouldn't have been such a good idea. I hear skunks taste horrible!

Pupp tried to bend the runner back into place, but it wouldn't budge. "Well kids," he sadly said, "This is going to slow us down. But we're not quitters, are we?"

All of us gave Pupp a deserving howl, telling him the race must go on. "Mush!" said Pupp, as we made our way back to the trail.

We were trying to make up for lost time, but snow covered directional markers and the wobble on the sled weren't helping. I was really wishing for a shortcut.

Soon after, Indy, with his keen discerning, informed me of thin ice on a small lake that the trail would cross. We slowed down and looked back at Pupp. He felt certain we were trying to tell him something, so he checked the map and clearly identified the lake. A few minutes later, Pupp shouted, "Gee!" for a right turn, and off the trail we began to travel, expecting a shortcut.

We had been running for hours, and then realized we had no idea where we were. Pupp said, "Easy…Whoa!" to stop us. Then he continued, "It won't be long before dark. This looks like a good spot to rest for the night."

At the same time, we could hear other dogs talking in the distance. Pupp said, "Let's go meet that other team. Maybe we can find out where we are."

The closer we got to those dogs, the more I recognized how familiar I was with one of those voices. As we closed in on them, they became quiet. *"Oh my goodness,"* I said, *"Mirage! What are you doing in the middle of the woods, tethered to three other dogs?"*

"Czarah, is that you?" Mirage said with excitement. *"Yes, it is you! It's so good to see you again! We are the Great Pennsylvania Sled Dog Race, Search and Rescue Team. I would love to chat and ask you how you've been, but we're lost and really need your help to locate the health station. Jazz was attacked and bitten by a rabid raccoon this morning, and our current owner has not cared for us properly with vet checks and rabies shots. We carry medical supplies on our driverless sled, but no vaccines of any kind,"* he claimed.

"Whoa! Slow down!" I said. *"None of you have had your rabies shots, and you're running around in the woods? That is so dumb! Anyway, we will help as much as we can. This morning's snow must have covered some of the signs,*

because we're lost too. We must put our noses together and find that health station," I announced.

"Hold on there. You can't plan on doing something different for somebody else in the middle of Pupp's race," said Neko.

It concerned me that Neko didn't want to help. Of course he didn't know these dogs, either.

"Neko," I said, *"If anyone or anything needs our assistance, we must help. Our temperament is: caring, kind, helping, loving, and very affectionate, among many more compassionate traits. We know Pupp wants to win this race, but we know Pupp wants to help. That's the kind of person he is. So, put winning out of your head and add some compassion for others instead."*

"Oh, and by the way," I continued, *"Kids, this is your Father. Mirage, these are your kids. You will learn their names later."*

I observed my children's wide-eyed faces and said, *"This is not a good time to discuss it."*

Pupp began to check each dog's collar for a nametag and said, "Hello Mirage, it sure is odd seeing you in the snow covered forest. I'm proud you made it to lead dog in search and rescue. This is a big accomplishment for you,

What did she just say?

congratulations! I see the remaining dogs' names are: Blake, Merlin, and our injured buddy, Jazz."

Pupp heard the kids whispering and continued, "Attention, everyone. I see there is some confusion here that I need to clarify. This dog is injured, and we, as a team, are going to see this through. They have a sound sled. Therefore, I will transport all of you and our cargo to their sled, get this dog the help he deserves and finish this race, together as a joined team. Please remember, the most important detail at heart is the safety and health of our family and friends. A race is just a race, but our family and friends are everything!"

First, Pupp tended to Jazz's wound with the medical

supplies they were carrying. Then he began to remove our cargo and place it into their sled. He detached Jazz from the gang line and placed him inside of a breathable cargo bag, located in the cargo bed. Pupp told him, "I know this is not where you want to be, but to keep you and everyone else safe from harm, this is where you must stay until we reach the health station."

Jazz grumbled a little, but understood and made himself comfortable.

"I'm not sure where we are going, but we can't just sit here. By looking at this map I'm going to take a guess and say we should go gee, then haw, then gee, then haw. Eventually, we'll come out of these woods. So, mush team, mush!" Pupp declared.

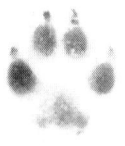

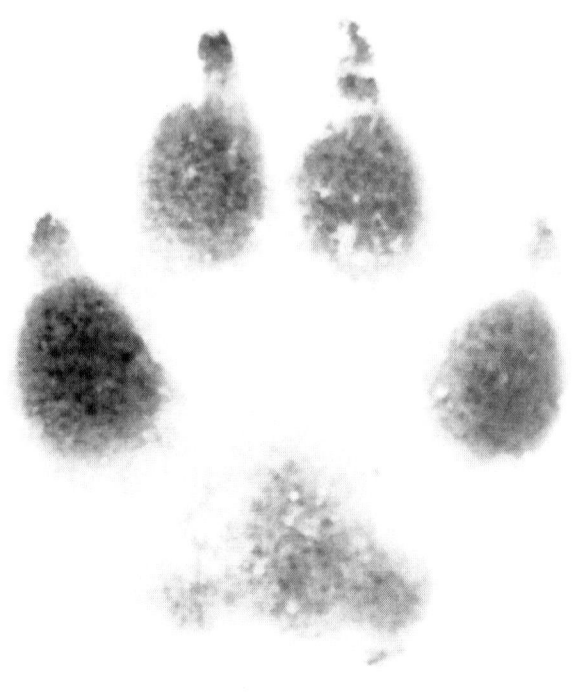

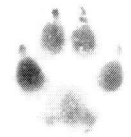

CHAPTER NINE
A MAGICAL EXPERIENCE

Mirage and I were side by side, leading the team. Right away we took a trip down memory lane and talked about events in our lives since we had last met at the dog show hotel. I started the conversation by saying, *"Well, here we are leading our children in a sled race. Isn't it odd that we meet again, out here in the middle of nowhere?"*

Mirage answered, *"Yes, it is. I suppose it's fate. Do you believe in fate?"*

"I don't know," I said. *"I'm not sure what fate is."*

"Well," Mirage explained, *"It's the same as destiny. In other words, fate put us together. I have no doubt that we crossed each other's path because we are destined to be together. I think about you often, Czarah."*

"I've thought of you many times, too," I replied.

I was beginning to feel that blushing again, so I quickly changed the subject. *"So, tell me how you managed to earn lead dog in your search and rescue team."*

Mirage explained, *"I was bought by a lady in southern Pennsylvania, east of Pittsburgh, who's an apprentice search and rescue trainer. It was easy for me because I already had show dog training. Mostly, I was guided alongside two of America's greatest teachers: Koyuk and Anevay. They had the ability to sense..."*

"What did you just say?" I shouted.

He repeated, *"I said, that they had the ability to..."*

"I know what you said. You said Koyuk and Anevay! They're my mother and great-grandmother. Your new owner is where I was born. Wow, it's a small world isn't it?" I explained.

"Yes, I suppose it is," he muttered, not wanting to announce Anevay's recent death.

Instantly, I broke off our chitchat and brought the team to a screeching halt as I focused at what looked like a white wolf at a fork in the path. It was hard to see the almost transparent white animal in the dusk of the day; it blended with the snow, except for the ice blue eyes.

For some reason I trusted the large creature when we were given a peculiar head nod as it lured us down the path to the left. Just before it vanished, the wolf appeared to be floating across the snow.

"Did you see that?" I asked Mirage.

"Yes, I did," he answered gingerly.

I asked the kids, *"Did you see the white wolf?"*

I heard replies of, *"Yes!"* and *"It sure was big!"*

Tikaani said, *"I hope it isn't hungry."*

"No Kaan, I don't think it's hungry. I sense it is navigating the proper direction," I explained.

Neko said nervously, *"I hope it's not leading us into a trap. There could be a whole pack waiting for us around the next corner."*

Mirage responded with, *"It's all right, Neko. We are close descendants of the wolf, and I give them credit for their intelligence and leadership of the wilderness. As long as we respect them in their country, there is no distress."*

Pupp also sensed the wolf was trying to tell us something and shouted, "Follow the white wolf, haw!"

Darkness came upon us fast, and the snow was blowing sideways in the wind. We could no longer see the path.

The white wolf.

Pupp instructed us to bed down under a patch of trees for the night. He carried Jazz, safely wrapped in his cargo bag, to the center of the pack and gently placed him on the ground. Then Pupp wrapped a blanket around himself and curled up beside us. "It's bedtime, kids. We need our rest," Pupp said with a yawn.

While Pupp slept, we took turns surrounding him with our bulky, warm, furry bodies, protecting him from the wind and cold.

Nearly thirty minutes before sunrise, Mirage woke me after the first pair of bird chirps. I shook off the snow, and then one by one, each dog awoke to shiver the white stuff away and roll on Pupp to wake him.

The sky was clear, and the stars were bright; it was a beautiful morning. Pupp said, "Good morning kids, and hello comet," as he gazed at the sky with his eyes wide open. We watched it slowly make its way to the opposite side of the earth. Suddenly, it took the shape of a white husky—or maybe it was a white wolf—just before vanishing beyond the mountain tops.

Shortly after Pupp assembled us to the sled, I heard that maternal voice again, just like the one from the last comet I saw. She spoke the same words.

"One dawn to one dusk, a gift of speech unites. Gain insight swiftly from protectors alike. One dawn to one dusk, on a voyage to seek. Trust keen insight, for you shall no longer speak."

Just then, my heart began to pound as I saw the white wolf approach us from the forest. It stopped, and then stood there, surveying us like a meat market, overshadowing the path so we couldn't pass. I stood erect in front of my pack to protect them. Mirage overlapped himself ahead of me to meet the wolf head on. We were silent and helpless, wondering what the wolf would do next. Then it directed us to follow it through the woods and onto an alternate path.

Once we were on the forged path, its focus was to creep closer and closer toward us, until I noticed that this wolf seemed very familiar to me. *"Well now, that's not a wolf at all. It's Anevay, my great-grandmother,"* I told the pack.

I tried to approach Anevay, to give her a hug and tell her I had missed her, but Mirage prevented me from doing so. He positioned himself in front of me like a concrete statue with eyes as big as saucers. We were harnessed together, so I couldn't move too much. Then he whispered to me, *"Czarah, she died months ago. She's not real."*

"Mirage," I said, *"She's not dead. She is standing right in front of me."*

When I looked to her, the rising sun had just broken ground and was reflecting off the snow. It was then that I noticed her transparency as I identified the forest trees through her body. Suddenly, I realized that I was about to speak to a ghost.

Anevay came in contact with me one last time by offering an affectionate nose rub to the side of my face. I will never forget her final words. *"Your life is perfect. You have everything and everyone you need. Therefore, my job here is done. I love you, my dear, and I will see you someday, beyond the Rainbow Bridge."*

 I told her, *"Goodbye, Anevay! I love you too!"* She smiled and quickly faded away, until all I could see was snow.

Pupp's mouth dropped when he saw the ghost. He stood there quietly as he understood every spoken word.

A few moments later, Pupp quietly asked, "Czarah, are you all right, honey?"

"Yes, I'm all right, Pupp. I know she is going to a beautiful place, and I will see her again," I told him.

"Czarah, I completely understood every word you and Anevay just said!" Pupp stated.

"What? That's impossible," I told him. *"You're imagining things. You're been subjected to the cold for too long."*

"No, it has nothing to do with being in the cold for too long," Pupp replied. "It's unbelievable, but I know exactly what you're saying."

"Wait, it's not impossible. Anevay said, 'One dawn to one dusk, a gift of speech unites.' This means we have speech for one whole day," I said.

I continued, "'Gain insight swiftly from protectors alike.' Anevay has been my protector. I have gained insight from her by obeying her direction. But Pupp, you're my protector too."

I extended my thoughts with, "'One dawn to one dusk, on a voyage to seek' is talking about this sled race we are in. This is our voyage to seek help for Jazz, Mirage, Merlin and Blake. It's to get their rabies shots so they don't die out here."

Then I said, "The last line was, 'Trust keen insight, for you shall no longer speak.' This must mean at some point we will no longer be able to speak to each other, but when?"

"So what do you think, Mirage? How long will we be able to speak?" I asked. He looked at me and whimpered. Mirage, Blake, Merlin and Jazz were unaware of what was happening. They could not speak.

"Great assessment, Czarah," Pupp said, "but I think we need to get going now. I trust Anevay has led us onto the path that will lead to the health station and the finish line. We can talk later. Believe me, I have many questions."

Immediately, we embarked on our journey, which took us three hours of swift running. "There's the health station, just beyond the finish line!" Pupp shouted unexpectedly. We hustled to a pace that seemed as though we were traveling as fast as the speed of light to cross that finish line. Pupp guided the team to the front door, lifted Jazz from the cargo bed, and carried him inside.

An hour later, Pupp approached the sled with the doctor and said, "Jazz will be fine. The doctor will give you boys the rabies shot you are required to have, and your owner will be fined for not maintaining your vaccinations."

While the doctor was giving the last shot, our big, kind hearted, sweet Tikaani thought he would get an enormous laugh for years to come as he leaned toward the doctor and said, "Thanks, Doc!" At the same time, I gave Kaan a swift jolt to his shin with my rear foot, to interrupt his hysterical comedy act.

Just as I thought, that doctor almost had a heart attack. Holding his chest, he slowly stepped back. With doubt in his voice, he asked Pupp, "Did you hear that?"

Pupp raised his eyebrows and with a sluggish look on his face, he said, "Hear what?"

"Your dog just said, 'Thanks, Doc!'" said the doctor.

"Doc," said Pupp, "I think you need some rest. You've been hanging around dogs too much."

The doctor shrugged his shoulders and together they entered the Health Station. After a few minutes, they returned with bowls of chow-chow, smothered in warm chicken broth, for everyone.

We ate well and then proceeded to the race judge to learn that we had finished in third place. Wow, after all we went through, we still managed to finish third. Unbelievable! Or is it?

While we said goodbye to Mirage, Jazz, Merlin, and Blake, we witnessed their owner upset about the hefty fine and veterinary bill she received. But after the doctor had a long talk with her about the importance of annual rabies shots, she departed from the race with her dogs, more aware of the consequences.

After the race, Pupp praised us for a magical experience. He couldn't wait to get us alone in the truck to interview us during our drive home.

When we arrived home, Mupp greeted us with big hugs, kisses, and cheer. She was amazed when she found out we were talking. Face to face, we mutually exchanged information for hours and learned many interesting facts about one another—such an immense amount that I could write another book.

Because of our great love for the outdoors, we moved our chit-chat to the backyard where Pupp built a raging fire to roast hot dogs for dinner. Shortly thereafter, a moment of silence came over us. We gazed at each other's glowing eyes and watched the reflections of fire sparks.

The sun was setting; another wonderful day had ended. Then suddenly, we could no longer talk. We still understood each other with single words and body language, but it sure had been nice to have that precious time to communicate face to face. I must say, so far, I do believe that this had been the best day of my life.

~

Six Months Later

~

We continue to howl and carry on conversations with one another. Sometimes Mupp and Pupp understand us, and sometimes they don't. I am now aware of the meaning connected with "trust keen insight" in the last sentence of Anevay's poem. It's not easy telling someone what you want when you can't speak. In the meantime, I'm already thinking of more questions to ask, if we are ever able to speak with a human voice again.

To this day, I believe Anevay portrayed herself as the comet, both times. That was her way of getting our attention. Obviously, it worked. Every night, I watch for comets and shooting stars, wishing for another chance to tell Anevay how much I love her, and maybe another opportunity to speak.

I know Anevay is proud of my pack and wants us to stay together, including Mirage. So, on occasion, Mupp and Pupp took me to visit him. And frequently, he came to visit us, until recently. On our last call to visit, Pupp said that the apprentice search and rescue trainer told him that Jazz had healed nicely. Then she said that their stunted team, excluding Mirage, continues to save lives of all ages. Pupp asked where he was, and she told him that he had been sold for profit and transported to Texas. When Pupp gave me the sad news that Mirage's owner had sold him, I was very disturbed, and will continue to be, until I know he is happy. But chances are I will never see him again.

As for sledding, it was quite an experience and the ideal adventure. But we decided to pull sleds around the house, romp, roll, and slide in the snow, and get involved with other things.

Chevy is training for search and rescue, when he's not amusing himself with the decoys. He truly loves to ambush his find with play. Then he thinks it's *his* turn to run and hide from the decoy.

Indy trained eagerly to pass the canine good citizenship and therapy dog exam. He is now a certified therapy dog and proudly visits day care centers, schools, nursing homes, and library reading programs. Like his father, he has also been qualified as a show dog and has currently won eleven awards.

Samarah likes to lie around and look beautiful following much deserved recognition due to her supermodel photos in numerous magazines. She had such an influence with one of the magazines that they photographed our entire pack and issued a centerfold article about our family. Just like she did with my previous winning photo, Mupp bought a magazine for all of their relatives.

Neko follows every move Indy makes. Therefore, he might pursue one of Indy's careers. He upholds the daily mole patrols as one of his night watchman duties, covering every square foot of our fenced-in yard.

Tikaani is an angel dressed as a Siberian husky. He's always ready to give hugs and kisses and continues to be an enormous eating machine. Often, you can find him in the kitchen studying Mupp and Pupp, trying to master the responsibilities of a chef and master taste tester.

Anevay has become a well-known guardian spirit. She is often seen all over the world, guiding lost pets back to their homes.

Me? My job is to keep everyone in line. I truly enjoy motherhood and wouldn't have it any other way. Every day is another adventure, or a lesson in life or love with my amazing family and friends. I must say, I'm very lucky to have this wonderful life. Often, I cry for mistreated dogs and those left outside to a chained life of unhappiness. Sometimes, life just isn't fair.

L.A. Adamson

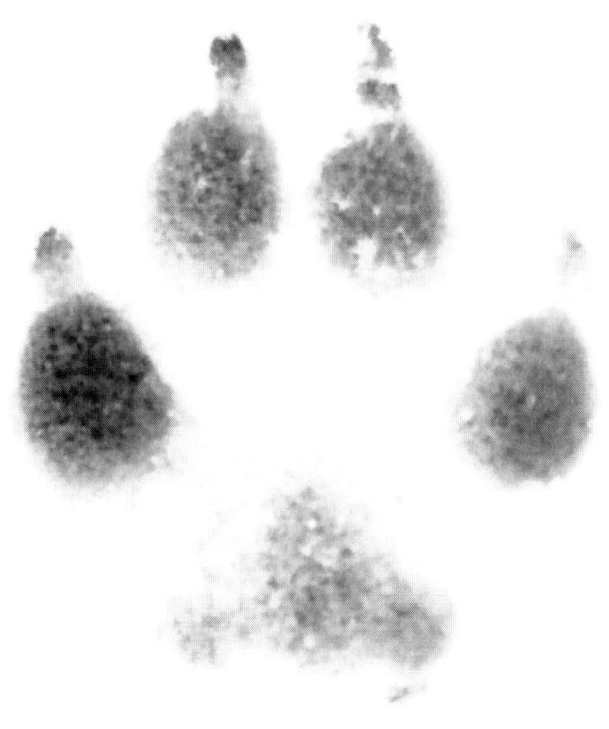

The Soggypaw Siberian Huskies ask that you spay and neuter your pets to prevent unwanted babies. There are too many living caged in shelters today. If you decide you want a pet, read about the breed you are interested in, for the reason that all breeds are different. And, please, please, please, save a life and adopt from your local shelter.

Learn more about Soggypaw Siberian Huskies at www.soggypaw.net, and find Soggypaw Siberian Huskies on Facebook.

A portion of this book's profit will be used to help animal shelters and to pay veterinary bills for those injured.

L.A. Adamson

Czarah Mae

Indy

L.A. Adamson

Chevy

Samarah

L.A. Adamson

Neko

Tikaani

Do you know how hard it is to get 6 Siberian huskies to sit still for a photo shoot? Here is 5 out of 6 with Samarah looking away and Tikaani missing in action.

The cover photo from a magazine we were featured in.

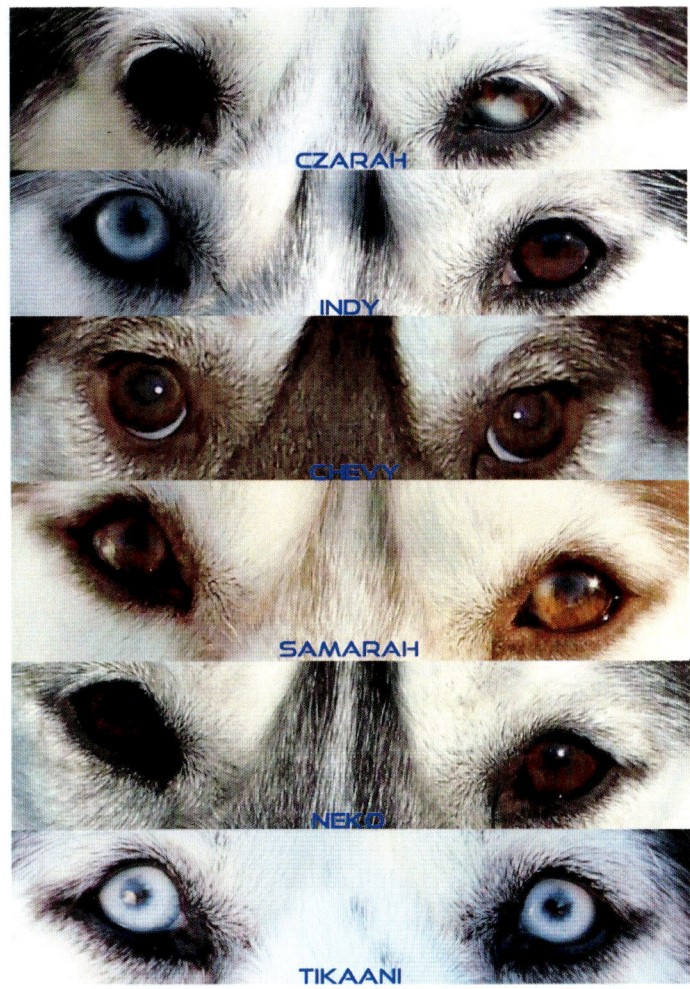